The Barnyard Bunch

PLAYFUL PIGS

Ryan James

Norwood House Press

Cataloging-in-Publication Data

Names: James, Ryan.
Title: Playful pigs / Ryan James.
Description: Buffalo, NY : Norwood House Press, 2026. | Series: The barnyard bunch | Includes glossary and index.
Identifiers: ISBN 9781978574359 (pbk.) | ISBN 9781978574366 (library bound) | ISBN 9781978574373 (ebook)
Subjects: LCSH: Swine--Juvenile literature. | Livestock--Juvenile literature.
Classification: LCC SF395.5 J359 2026 | DDC 636.4--dc23

Published in 2026 by
Norwood House Press
2544 Clinton Street
Buffalo, NY 14224

Designer: Rhea Magaro
Editor: Kim Thompson

Photo credits: Cover, p. 1 Clara Bastian/Shutterstock.com; p. 5Ewa Studio/Shutterstock.com; p. 6 2xSamara.com/Shutterstock.com; p. 7 AlbHen/Shutterstock.com; p. 8 Eric Isselee/Shutterstock.com; p. 9 Matthew J Thomas/Shutterstock.com; p. 10 UbjsP/Shutterstock.com; p. 11 Filmbildfabrik/Shutterstock.com; p. 12 Pavle Bugarski/Shutterstock.com; p. 15 Goldenxxboy/Shutterstock.com; p. 16 Wirestock Creators/Shutterstock.com; p. 17 Sean Fleming/Shutterstock.com; p. 18 Kitreel/Shutterstock.com; p. 19 talseN/Shutterstock.com; p. 21 LeManilo/Shutterstock.com;

Printed in the United States of America

CPSIA compliance information: Batch #CSNHP26: For further information contact Norwood House Press at 1-800-237-9932.

TABLE OF CONTENTS

PLAYFUL PIGS

Pigs are farm animals. They live in the barnyard.

HOW PIGS LOOK

Most **domesticated** pigs have short hair. Their hair comes in many colors.

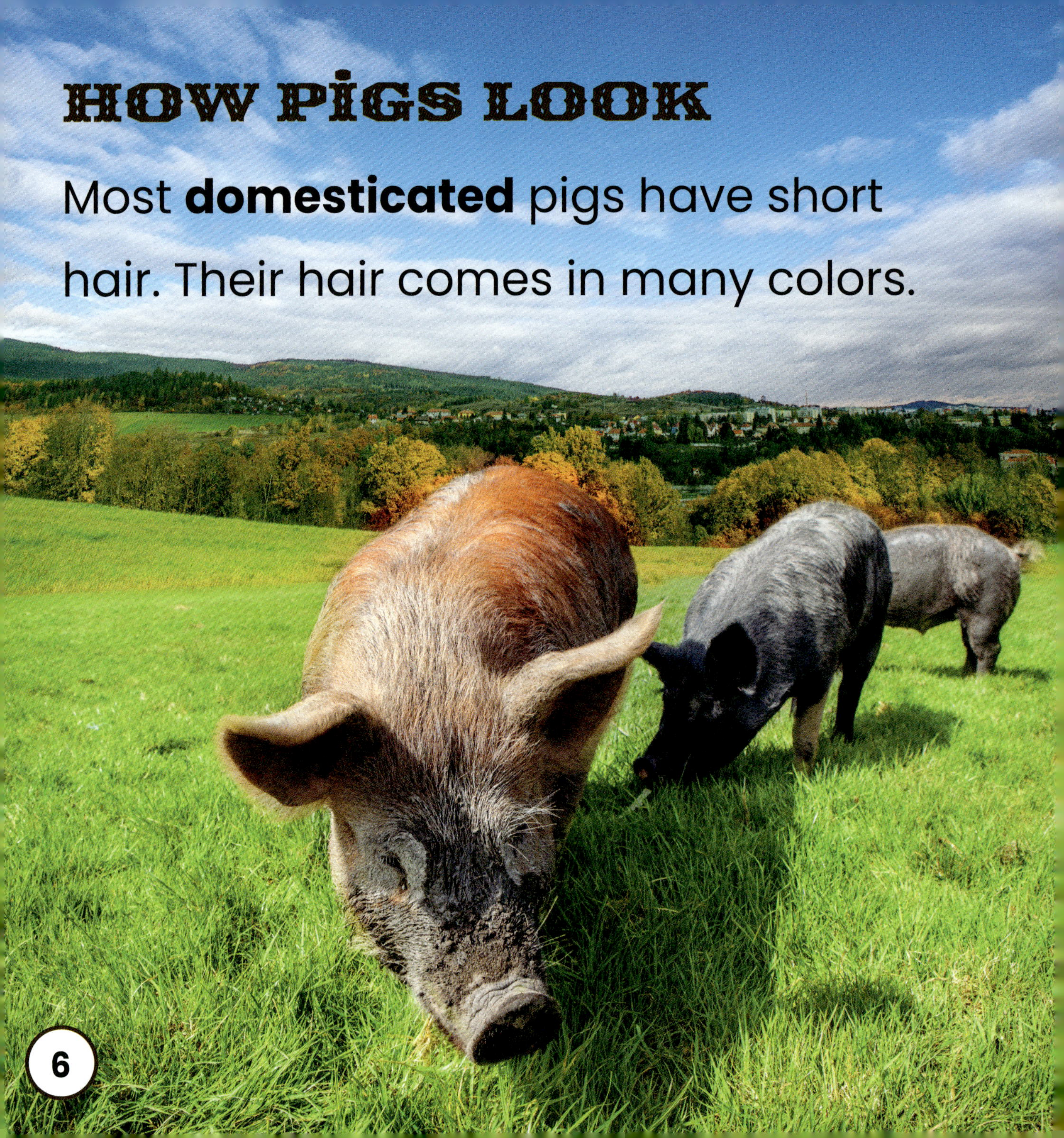

Pigs have thick skin. This helps them stay warm.

Pigs have four legs with **hooves**.

A pig's **snout** is very **sensitive**. It uses its snout to smell and **root** for food.

HOW PIGS SOUND

Pigs make different types of **grunts**.

They use grunts to **communicate** with other pigs.

Pigs squeak when they are excited.
They scream when they are in trouble.

WHAT PIGS EAT

Pigs are **omnivores**. They like to eat all kinds of food.

Farmers feed pigs **grains**.

Pigs also eat fruits and vegetables.

They even eat insects!

HOW PIGS GROW UP

Baby pigs are called piglets. Mother pigs teach piglets new things.

Piglets learn to cool off by rolling in the mud.

FUN ON THE FARM

Pigs are **intelligent**. They like to play and run around. Sometimes, they lie in the sun.

GLOSSARY

communicate (kuh-MYOO-ni-kate): to share information and feelings

domesticated (duh-MES-ti-kay-tid): not wild; lives on farms or with people

grains (graynz): cereal plants such as wheat, corn, and oats

grunts (gruhnts): short, low sounds

hooves (hoovz): hard parts that cover the feet of pigs, horses, and other animals

intelligent (in-TEL-i-juhnt): quick to learn and understand; smart

omnivores (AHM-nuh-vorz): animals that eat both plants and meat

root (root): to poke or dig about

sensitive (SEN-si-tiv): able to sense small changes and differences

snout (snout): the long front part of an animal's head that includes the nose, mouth, and jaws

THINKING QUESTIONS

1. What are baby pigs called?

2. How does a pig's snout help it?

3. What do pigs eat?

4. How do pigs communicate?

5. What do pigs enjoy doing on the farm?

INDEX

ABOUT THE AUTHOR

Ryan James lives in the mountains of North Carolina, where he goes hiking with his dog Bailey. He loves fly fishing, visiting farms in the area, and picking fresh produce. He has always enjoyed writing and wrote his first book as a teenager.